Pirates

Andrew Langley
Consultant: Richard Tames

Miles Kelly
PUBLISHING

First published in 2002 by
Miles Kelly Publishing Ltd
Bardfield Centre, Great Bardfield, Essex, CM7 4SL

Some material in this book can also be found in *100 Things You Should Know About Pirates.*

Editor: Amanda Learmonth

Design: Debbie Meekcoms

Index: Lynn Bresler

Art Director: Clare Sleven

Editorial Director: Paula Borton

British Library Cataloguing-in-Publication Data
A catalogue record for this book is available from the British Library

ISBN 1-84236-107-4

Printed in Hong Kong

www.mileskelly.net
info@mileskelly.net

ACKNOWLEDGEMENTS

The Publishers would like to thank the following artists who have contributed to this book:

Peter Dennis (Linda Rogers Assoc.), Nicholas Forder, Mike Foster (Maltings Partnership), Terry Gabbey (AFA), Luigi Galante (Studio Galante), Sally Holmes, Richard Hook (Linden Artists Ltd), Kevin Maddison, Janos Marffy, Alessandro Menchi (Studio Galante), Terry Riley, Pete Roberts (Allied Artists), Martin Sanders, Mike White (Temple Rogers)

Computer-generated cartoons by James Evans

Contents

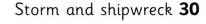

The pirate's world

A pirate is a robber on the sea. Pirates attack ships and ports, stealing treasure and other valuables. As soon as the first ships began to carry goods, pirates began to plunder (steal from) them. Pirates are still a threat today.

The Barbarossa brothers were famous pirates who came from North Africa.

Buccaneers were originally criminals and pig hunters.

Privateers were given permission to attack ships from enemy countries.

5

Sea raiders

Ancient Greece was home to some of the earliest-known pirates. From around 500BC, there were many cargo ships trading along the Mediterranean coasts, which were often raided by pirates. A few centuries later, the Vikings arrived on the coast of Britain in search of riches and adventure.

▶ Vikings from the North raided settlements on the British coast. They terrified Britons with their fierce weapons.

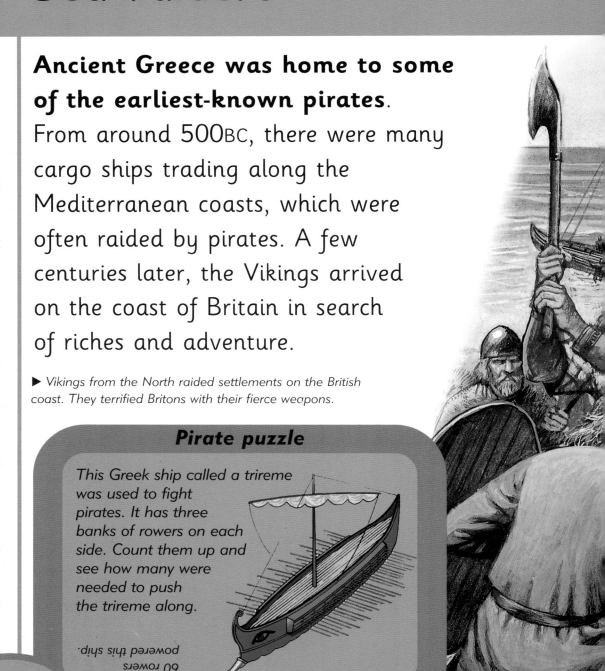

Pirate puzzle

This Greek ship called a trireme was used to fight pirates. It has three banks of rowers on each side. Count them up and see how many were needed to push the trireme along.

60 rowers powered this ship.

Ancient pirate ships were small and fast so they could escape easily.

Roman cargo ships sailed close to the coast, so it was easier for pirates to attack them.

Viking longships were narrow so they could land almost anywhere.

Cruel corsairs

Pirates of the Mediterranean were known as 'corsairs'.
The most famous corsairs were Muslims from the Barbary Coast of North Africa. They took great delight in plundering Christian ships. They wanted people, not treasure, so that they could sell them as slaves.

Patch Jack's fun facts!

The famous Barbarossa brothers were so-called because of their red beards – *Barba rossa* means 'Redbeard' in Latin.

▲ A musketoon had a wide end, or muzzle, so that when it was fired, the shot was spread out.

A scimitar was a curved sword used by the corsairs.

Grenades were thrown on to the ship to set it on fire.

A dagger was small enough to hide under clothes for a surprise attack!

Spanish invaders

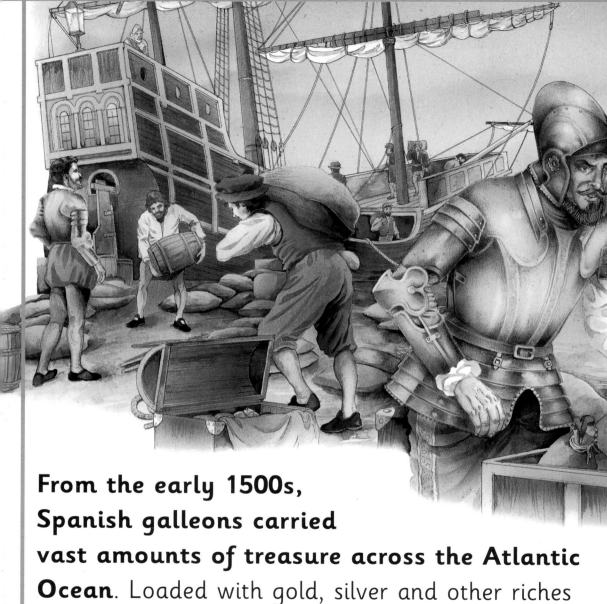

**From the early 1500s,
Spanish galleons carried
vast amounts of treasure across the Atlantic
Ocean**. Loaded with gold, silver and other riches
from Central and South America, these huge
ships attracted pirates like bees to a honeypot.

Francis le Clerc was a fierce pirate known as 'Peg Leg' because of his wooden leg.

Ancient riches like this gold knife were found in the Americas.

▲ These soldiers were called *conquistadors*. They were the first Spanish soldiers to invade the 'Spanish Main', or Central and South America.

Patch Jack's fun facts!

When Christopher Columbus, the Italian explorer, first landed in the Americas, he thought he had found Asia!

Attacking the enemy

Some sailors were given permission to attack ships from enemy countries. This could only happen if they carried a special letter from their king or queen. These sailors did not call themselves pirates, but were known as 'privateers'. Privateering mostly took place between the 16th and 18th centuries.

▲ Francis Drake, a famous privateer, raided Spanish settlements in Panama, Central America. He once attacked a mule train carrying silver.

Walter Raleigh was beheaded by James I for returning from two voyages empty-handed.

Francis Drake was a great privateer, who brought back many riches from all over the world.

▲ Some privateers captured slaves and sold them in exchange for gold, silver and pearls.

Patch Jack's fun facts!

A ship would raise its country's flag to other passing ships. So privateers often raised a fake flag to an enemy ship to pretend they were friendly!

Bold buccaneers

Buccaneers were pig hunters and criminals who had settled on the island of Hispaniola (modern Cuba). The Spanish tried to drive them away, so the buccaneers banded together and started attacking passing Spanish merchant ships.

▼ The buccaneers invented a special kind of sword – the cutlass. They carried it as their main weapon in battle.

Henry Morgan started out as a privateer, but soon became a famous buccaneer.

Pirate puzzle

There are six pirate weapons hidden in this picture.

Can you find a scimitar, a dagger, a pistol, a musketoon, a battle axe and a firebomb?

A battle axe was used to cut down the sails of the enemy ship.

A pistol was light and easy to carry during an attack.

15

Ocean of thieves

Pirates sailed the Indian Ocean for many centuries. They were attracted by the exotic treasures of the East, such as silks, spices and jewels. Pirate ships lay in wait along the Indian coast, seizing the cargoes of lone merchant ships as they passed.

Pirate search!

The surnames of five pirates and privateers are hidden in this letter square.

Can you find them all?

B	R	N	A	D	C	X	M
D	R	A	K	E	B	N	O
L	E	C	L	E	R	C	R
K	R	K	S	E	S	W	G
L	O	I	A	A	I	G	A
D	S	D	N	L	S	G	N
C	Y	D	T	E	A	C	H

Drake, Raleigh, Morgan, Le Clerc, Kidd

▼ *The large island of Madagascar was wild and unexplored, so it was easy for pirates to hide there.*

William Kidd *was sent to chase pirates in the Indian Ocean but soon became a pirate himself!*

Precious jewels *such as rubies and emeralds were taken from passing Indian ships.*

Henry Avery, *known as the 'Arch Pirate', captured the Indian Emperor's treasure ship.*

17

Pirates of the East

The South China Sea was the perfect place for pirates. There were lots of small islands, swamps and narrow channels to hide in, and many merchant ships to attack. Chinese pirates became famous for their violence and brutal methods.

▲ *The Strait of Malacca was one of the many channels that attracted pirates.*

Test your memory!

1. Who were the two most feared corsairs?
2. What was pirate Francis le Clerc known as?
3. What is the name of the pirates who lived on the island of Hispaniola, modern Cuba?

1. the Barbarossa brothers 2. Peg Leg 3. buccaneers

◄ Chinese pirates sailed in ships called junks. The sails were made from bamboo.

A kris (left) was a kind of sword used by Eastern pirates. The scabbard (right) was its wooden case.

Chinese pirates led a harsh life on board, with little more to eat than boiled rice.

Women pirates

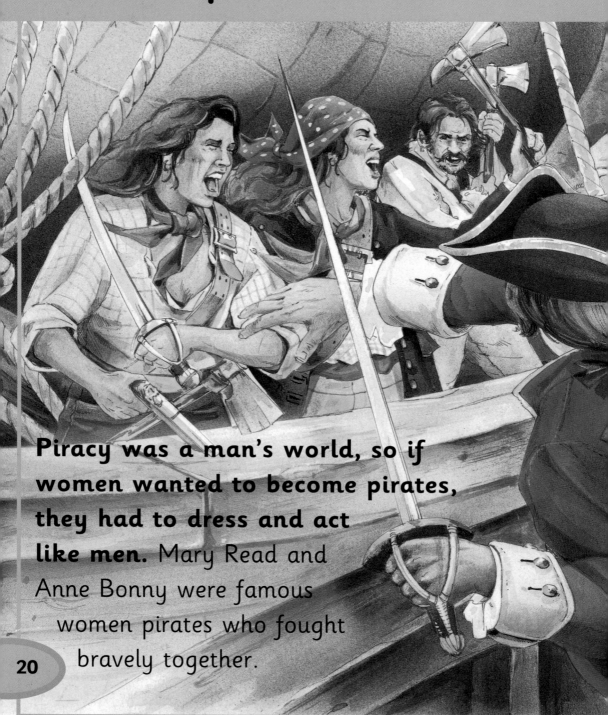

Piracy was a man's world, so if women wanted to become pirates, they had to dress and act like men. Mary Read and Anne Bonny were famous women pirates who fought bravely together.

Grace O'Malley commanded a pirate fleet in Ireland.

Ching Shih took over her husband's pirate fleet after his death.

Patch Jack's fun facts!

Grace O'Malley cut her hair short to look like her sailors. This earned her the nickname of 'Baldy'!

Life on board

Most pirate ships had to be small and fast. On the Spanish Main, most were 'schooners' with two masts, or galleys with three masts. Below deck, there was not much space for the crew to sleep. The food was mostly horrid – dry biscuits and pickled meat was often all there was to eat.

Dress as a pirate

1. Tie a red scarf round your head.
2. Put on trousers, shirt and waistcoat.
3. Put on earrings.
4. Make your own black moustache out of wool.
5. Make an eyepatch from cardboard and elastic bands.
6. Now all you need is a blood-curdling pirate yell!

Foresail

Foremast

Bowsprit

Bow (front)

Mizzen topsail

Main topsail

Fore topsail

Mainsail

Stern
(back)

Sail locker

Water and
stores

Oars

The stern
(back) was
where the
captain's cabin
was found.

The sail locker
kept the sails
dry when they
weren't in use.

The bowsprit
supported the
foremast and
foresail.

▲ A galley was one of the larger pirate ships. It was powered
by sail and wind, or by oar if there was no wind.

23

Pirate attack

Pirates depended on speed to catch their victims. If they had cannon, they would try to hit the other ship's rigging (its sails and mast) to slow the ship down. When they were near enough, the pirates threw hooked ropes into the rigging to catch the ship. They then climbed on board.

Design a pirate flag

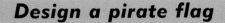

On a black background, draw your own scary design using bones, skulls, swords and anything else you fancy.
Now you have your very own pirate flag!

Bartholomew Roberts, or Black Bart, was probably one of the most successful pirates ever.

▼ One of the best ways to slow a ship was to fire at the sails.

Pirate flags were raised when a pirate ship decided to attack. This was done to frighten the victims.

Treasure pleasure

All pirates dreamed of gold and silver.
Some were lucky enough to capture ships packed
with them – in the form of coins, gold bars or
finely made ornaments. But most merchant
ships carried simpler goods, such as cloth,
coal or iron.

◀ *People too
could be valuable.
Pirates might
capture a rich
person and
demand money
from his relatives.
When this was
paid, the prisoner
was freed.*

Patch Jack's fun facts!

*When
goods were
difficult to sell,
pirates dumped
them overboard.
One beach was said
to be ankle-deep
in precious
spices!*

Pieces of eight
were valuable
coins brought
back from the
Spanish Main.

Treasure chests
were often full
of jewellery,
ornaments and
fine materials
such as silk.

The crew
would wait
eagerly as the
captain shared
out the goods.

▲ After capturing a
cargo ship, the pirates took all
the treasure to their own ship.

27

Castaway!

If a pirate broke the rules on board ship, he was punished by being left alone on a deserted island. This was called marooning. He was given a few important things – water, a pistol and gunpowder. It was almost impossible to escape, and food was often hard to find.

A castaway was a pirate left all alone on a desert island.

▲ Alexander Selkirk was stranded on a desert island for five long years. The story *Robinson Crusoe* by Daniel Defoe is based on Selkirk's real-life adventures.

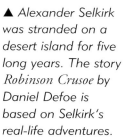

Fresh water soon ran out, so the castaway had to find his own.

Patch Jack's fun facts

The famous castaway, Alexander Selkirk, kept himself busy on his desert island by teaching wild cats and goats to dance!

Storm and shipwreck

Shipwreck was a pirate's biggest nightmare. Violent storms could spring up suddenly, driving helpless ships on to a rocky shore. The pirates had to find their way across the sea by skill and luck, using special equipment to help them.

Test your memory!

1. Where on a galley ship was the stern?
2. What are pieces of eight?
3. What is the name of a pirate who is left on a desert island?
4. What is the book based on Alexander Selkirk's adventures called?

1. at the back 2. coins
3. a castaway
4. Robinson Crusoe

A compass was used to show which direction the ship was moving.

A telescope helped pirates to spot land in the distance.

Dividers were used by pirates to measure distances on maps.

Pirate hunters

European countries began to build bigger and stronger navies.
With these, they were able to begin fighting off the pirates. Pirates were offered free pardons if they gave up their lives of crime. Large rewards were given to anyone who helped to capture pirate ships.

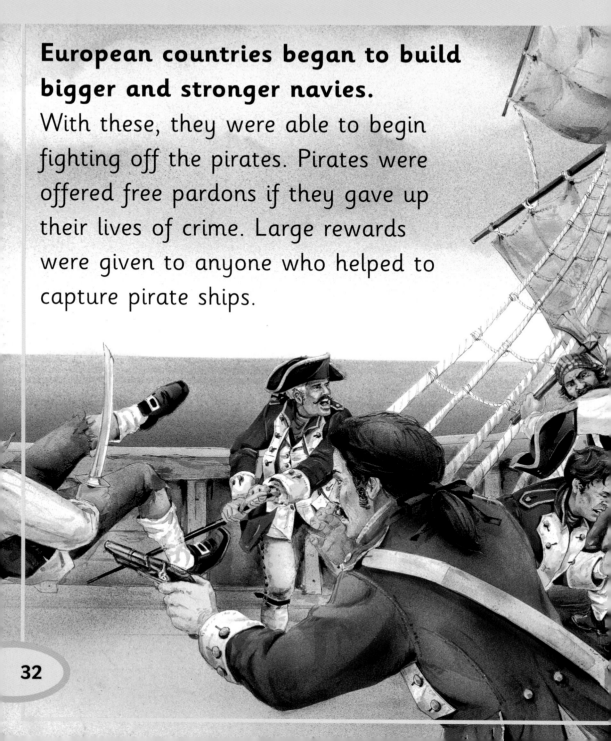

Pirate puzzle

Which pirate names do these
pictures make you think of?

A

B

D

C

A. Barbarossa ('Red-beard') brothers
B. Francis 'Peg-leg' Le Clerc
C. Grace 'Baldy' O'Malley **D.** Blackbeard

Navy officers
were well
armed to fight
the pirates.

Blackbeard
was one of the
most terrifying
pirates.

**Robert
Maynard,**
a naval officer,
finally killed
Blackbeard.

33

Pirate punishment

Many captured pirates were taken back to Britain in chains. But most never got that far. They were taken to the nearest port and executed as quickly as possible. Only the younger criminals of 15 or 16 years old were pardoned and released.

▼ *This is one of the dreaded 'hulks'. These were old naval ships that were used as floating prisons for the worst criminals.*

▲ Before and after trial, the pirates were
kept in prison. Prisons were brutal and
unhealthy places, where prisoners
often died of disease
or starvation.

Prisoners
*were chained
together to
stop them
escaping.*

An iron cage
*displayed the
pirate's dead
body to warn
anyone who
might become
a pirate!*

Patch Jack's fun facts!

*After one
pirate was hanged,
someone saw that
he was still
breathing! Luckily
for him, he was
let off and sent
to Australia
instead.*

Pirates today

Pirates are not a thing of the past. There are still plenty of pirates on the seas today. Modern-day pirates move in at the dead of night in small boats, and climb up ropes on to the decks of merchant ships. It only takes them a few minutes to steal all the valuables on board, slip over the side again and disappear into the dark.

Map quiz

Where on the map did each of these pirates base their pirate attacks?

1. The Spanish *conquistadors*　**2.** The buccaneers
3. William Kidd　**4.** The corsairs

UNITED KINGDOM
London
USA
ATLANTIC SPAIN
OCEAN Mediterranean
Sea
CHINA
PACIFIC
OCEAN
HISPANIOLA (CUBA)
Malacca
Straits
SOUTH
AMERICA
INDIAN
OCEAN
PACIFIC
OCEAN
MADAGASCAR AUSTRALIA

1. South America 2. Hispaniola (Cuba) 3. Indian Ocean 4. Mediterranean Sea

Today's pirates use stealth, meaning they sneak quietly on to the ships.

Modern weapons like machine guns are used.

Small boats let the pirates get as close as possible to the ship.

37

Playful pirates

Many of us get our ideas of pirates from reading books or watching films.

The best-known pirate of all – Long John Silver – is in a story book. This one-legged pirate appears in Robert Louis Stevenson's *Treasure Island*. Captain Hook is another famous pirate, from *Peter Pan*. There are cartoon pirates too, such as the jolly Captain Pugwash.

▼ A scene from Robert Louis Stevenson's *Treasure Island*. You can see Long John Silver with his parrot, the wild castaway Ben Gunn, and, of course, the treasure!

▲ *The Pirates of Penzance* is an operetta by Gilbert and Sullivan. The pirates in this are kind-hearted and jolly.

Captain Hook has his hand cut off by hero Peter Pan, so the captain has a hook instead.

Robert Louis Stevenson wrote *Treasure Island*, one of the best-loved adventure stories.

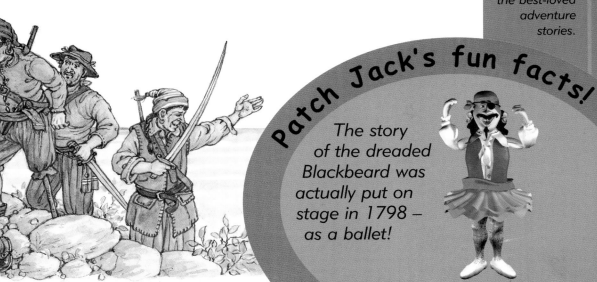

Patch Jack's fun facts!

The story of the dreaded Blackbeard was actually put on stage in 1798 – as a ballet!

Index